APOLOGIES

Kristin P. Bradshaw

APOLOGIES

Burning Deck/Anyart, Providence

Acknowledgments:

The author wishes to thankfully acknowledge *No: A Journal of the Arts* and *Chase Park*, where some of these poems first appeared in print, and Ben Marcus and Ange Mlinko, editors of the online journal *impossible object*, where very early versions of "19" and "28" were both posted as "Untitled".

Special thanks for enduring support or influence to Melissa Van Doren Weaver, Sarah Gambito, Kathleen Andersen, CD Wright, Forrest Gander, Anna N. Williams, Peter S. Hawkins, MK Guth, Christian DiMenna, Luis Martins, Karen Carmean, Bobbie and Toby Bradshaw, and Kate Copeland.

Cover by the author

Burning Deck is the literature program of Anyart: Contemporary Arts Center, a tax-exempt (501c3), non-profit organization.

ISBN13: 978-1-936194-19-3, original paperback

APOLOGIES: DRAFTS 1—73

for Keith Waldrop
and for Sarah Gambito

credo quia absurdum est
[I believe because it is absurd]
—Tertullian

Experience is one of the forms of paralysis.
—Erik Satie, *Ecrits* [via John Cage]

I have never, with respect to myself, thought while writing that I was a woman. This may have been a shock to many women—but I do not write as a woman, I write as a writer, insofar as I am able to write. Which means that for me there is no difference between a text written...by a man or a text written by a woman.
—Anne-Marie Albiach, *A Discursive Space* [trans. Norma Cole]

PreFace

Dear Sir I have known you a million books.

An I acts out in turns
each refraction of a Self:

moving temples.

in the psychic garden, three maidens:
Ardent, Inquisitive, and Impassive—
I listened as each spoke to me in turns,
but then they mingled verses and no one
said what they were supposed to say

                                    nor when

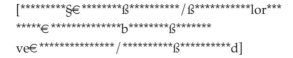

and this effusion became quite perplexing,
as if in a bar or a crowd of people,
so I picked up Virginia Woolf
                        but she too said all sorts of   things
                        things I could not believe like:

                        Shall I harangue,
                        You Sloth.

and finally, the motion going
onward, I picked up a notebook
so all voices would yield

stop
         directly before the pen moves

       *   *   *

there was one.

we ate nutmeg

or people watching their own performance

and like all accounts   is partial lie.

AVGVSTVS MMII   behind the
prosopon   the faces of

personae,

the schema skips sequence according to fragment, to
instances and   then accumulates

without every number as a touchstone—for some
there can be no apology.

1

Charlemagne   hold fast your spurs
ceaseless wind   horse writhing.
you, in shingled hut, wrapped in earth,
say for us that prayer or
dare it not cross your lips:
mold us not into fear;
lead us not into the weary Old Jerusalem.

moonshine riddles. my bed
in dark dust   when I learned that
man is no god   even in credence.
He believes often

                    a fire.

cold in a mild winter—
signs of progressive heart disease   much less.

to think we built roads by which to call ourselves barbarians,
as if we could implode.

And so a blessing:
Dante, I do not like the smell of shit.
          the word asshole.
          and yet for your glittering celestial rose, beatific but
One   indivisible union—
in domestic sign, Aristotle and I go our ways.
the drumming head   cleft.

We have our signature inks
but now the bone.

2

First sobriety: damning guise.
the bone in my left thigh
altered   swings freely.
a proverbial might say *wine will make*
you think what   you ought not think.
spiraling hues through vatic elixirs —
I mean to say the spiritual swoon, though
liquid, not invariably
liquid—word turns solid air.
                              at the marriage
ceremony, groom slaughtered
pig. belly meat & feast to follow. the men as thick
into blood   a tar concoction
boiled by earlier Americans: though not alcohol, still
proven hallucinogenic.

if Darwin had lived longer perhaps
the evolutionary process would have stopped
or, conceivably, in some leather notebook
is scribbled *manipulate the monkeys Amen.*

Swilling shots of schnapps   reminiscent
of the old apartment. moldings laced with
brown cobwebs where in summer
heat stripped the tawny wallpaper. heat
the weight of 13, 428 cockroaches seen
in the kitchen alone.

Let me tell you of the Spirit
Charming.

Shall I croon badly to you;
would I be a raucous fellow?

3

Dear Friend— I am mutely sitting and thinking of you yet
still I have not sent my last letter, or the
one before and a postcard. We have a new
plant   named <u>Yeller Mule</u>

Get up, Mule.

From the interstate our house   indistinguishable among
the rooftops. Little soil, here I have learned
something about spaces   *now you are gone.*
Paris is not far from me. Graciously.

4

In the painting: I am not the same man
as my father. What god would choose
to make me in its image? barren, the sea.
Once carpentered, sailing vessels
now sport fiberglass hulls. And horses too
for frolic   carrying histrionic suns around
the window at a predestined arc. mounting
misfortunes conquer the hills   except for
the green tailed Two-Inch Squirrels. [or] a road
to name my uncle by, the chicken pen and dogs.
mahogany earth spots filled with water
and the women there with sodden skirts.

Peter Abelard, you are among my favorite castrated
heroes. A real castrato — that night I bet they made you sing.
As for inks, their faint permanence
yields no comfort for my doubting
Thomas, no Sister Heloise.

I am not a woman according to the definition.

The monastery father allowed only a pair
of sandals. Winter one: lost my toes and could not walk
away. The others routinely soiled the sheep.
Upon finding what I did not have and
what I was not and was and of all the corrupt seeds
sown here,
          I am standing in the greatest stench.

6

I have heard you many nights
proclaim my meanness   Mother
And how exacting to
remember where I left boot tracks last summer.

8

Sister, things come to me quite slowly.
Forgive me, my attempts to reach you fail
as ever   and though current graphics
reveal the lunar landscape desolate,
I'm quite convinced that all things squandered
are buried on the moon.

ocean   reducible to symbol.

                              by study we
                              talk of Platonic formalism

  table   not Table Form
                   ∴

i   not Human Form

Adams perhaps   (but questionably)
subject to decay   [addiction] this human.

we see more i in cigarette
                         [and]
there is no *me* in
          de casibus virorum illustrium
the fall of great men   we have not transpired.

I thought Cardinal and wished to be educated.
I met a pope   another *distinctive of*
ecclesiastical or academic station.

I dreamt rustic violence: shot a bear, lost a dog,
and I kissed you. Casanova in my fantasies   (what is not).

9

perhaps like *Murphy*, I am now and always
have been sitting in this rocking chair.

Upon finding myself posed
on the bottom of Fortuna's Wheel:
The River Thames jetting sick waves,
A virus decimates our village—a thing
passing through rose-lined pockets.
The Black Robes and burnings
carry our parents like wind. I am a Parisian
child in a room with Nostradamus   he
tells me that I will die and live again
in a sable time. I do, as a London boy—
stacks of sooty sky. It is Blake now the
prophet   he says I will live forever in ebony
ink but *William, I do not want more lives.*

1949, my brother already engineering
cars, though a child, and I watch womenfolk
scrape the Georgia dirt for tobacco and corn.
The high sheriff runs the gristmill, the cows
flatulent July storms. Mamas   making
chicken and dumplings. I'm given bone,
the marrow spelling out a gospel:
                                The world
will be my playground. I will live
in a house with plumbing; marry a soldier,
divorce; marry a better man with two daughters.
we will have a third who will confuse things
in their beauty—Promethean struggle. And in a letter
to a wizened poet she will say: Dear Sir,
I am surrounded by a vernacular in which
I must engage   regretfully.

10 ^{through} 12

12601   high

> here in our John Muir Wilderness

j'attends comme toujours
c'était bleu et pleine
et toi   tu es

deposits pooling lake rust

> why salt permits a Q or any other letter

upper and lower petite zones

> incomparable   waving lines
> to the Sierra ridges

there also a solace in blue heat

10600   down

little French written

je te vois à côté de moi.

we have four gables

> our feet beneath us

he stands with a height tonight

it grows somber here expeditiously

11676

runnels

[marginal dyslexia]
Christian, lay your Burden down

[ah]

vast the afternoons, that they were

14

Love has pitched his mansion in
The place of excrement
—"Crazy Jane Talks with the Bishop," W. B. Yeats

longing cleric: some men become
basilicas, plow hands, the essence of letters.
Bartered talent for a hammer, for a map,
for a lamppost, for blue elevations—
assembling architecture through
a lover: contradiction   in agreement.

I am   a haphazard stack of shingles and boards,
copper fixtures, the toilet   erecting an
edifice with exterior piles: impervious materials.

Wilfred Owen, I dream of you in
rainy Summers.   how he must have intuited
an end to trench-life while enduring
the lime lined pits   not
enduring.
                    suffer Job, remain
inside us   moving temples.
Πιστις (pistis)   posy my pistol tongue burgeoning onward

15

She wants a candle devoid of mendacity—what light so often yields:

Query the old queen of fairies
whose solace is but mirage:
(a sans serif **Q** black on the forearm); same records
over again; [or] she could discover the street life with its streaks
of faces against blurred hues. red/green. too bright under the lamp post
and too dark in the alley.

steadily you encroach upon my reason.

bodies

marked by caliginous movements.

i offer no apology.

17

You want me to invoke you

    you, you hasty muse

what I see   banana bread and spinach

There is the lunch
I ate and other specifics,

          what I
tried to pen yesterday and the day before.

This is what I name nothing.

Nothing assembles.

19

What is the
requirement I said
Please give
answers   No
Percival my dear   I
am the woman
lover not the
chalice—the glass
spilt one
part wine to
two parts other

20

As if the brain could chose its neuroroutes—to remember
from under a pickling spell
that blue room before the sun...

A boy is in the bathroom; water like heavy machinery.

21

where is that portal, oh give me
liberty or a fatal blow

the sea is high and pitch at peaks
for pale but thick marauders, you: Angles, Saxons, Jutes.

coming, coming onslaught
lay open to new worlds.
(i feel it)

                                             emerald isles and emerald isles.

22

I felt Guinivere on my shoulders.
Error, we are balsam   beaches crumbling out.
ne'er the wind is blowing, ne'er against my shudders.
I know it has been left of me for some time now but
still does he love me or
have I hastened. when I look
my hand is ash spread out against the blight.
were you the air choked in alphabets and tongues

[or]

One might use this word *perhaps* to convey
uncertainty   to pick and pervert the laws in Leviticus.
I am Paris and you shall stride along the alleys of my personage
forever   and never, the difference is slight.
This is how short wits become—
codex of prosody and prostitution.

23

Goodnight Martha   give me the
bourbon bottle. insecurities need
a larger body   [or] no visible mole.
O Gertrude how you kiss kiss kiss
in all unreachable places. We laugh
maniacally when we think
of liquor drinks and summer.
Any mouth   can expound upon any
matter, but not any mouth on all.
Regretfully, a vernacular.
With his clothes off I see he is related
to gorillas. To think we call ourselves civilians
[the plight of rubrics]. He could easily be contented,
or so the tongue says—what makes a folk pariah?

ah, Galilean / Galileo of our azure orb.

Will you think of me   occasionally   I think of nothing:
I am   outside   and the rain like Charlemagne.

24

At the well she nourished our camels, her body casting
a rill of water

Rebekah
> *you were like a gift to us that winter*

abandoned on all sides by the most exquisite creatures

> *If you could hear me*

25

Ever present face in the door jamb.

                let the flood curve
                swaying back, back to Rowan Oak   [or]

she should not act like a Virginia gentleman.
the i of many cocktails:
                so many hours
                                will not transpire.

26

I, too, will sing of war when this matter of a girl is exhausted.
—*Homage to Sextus Propertius*, Ezra Pound

are you to fix that statement? or am I
to sit here pondering the gulf between
your meaning and mine?

infused with amicable intention, a banana was grace that day.

but after the great surge of excitement, i am left
to my own devices, entropic, like a fool

who wishes
for finesse and grace, for the paths
of least resistance.

27

Her hands, two great galleons skirting edge 'round
the table. he, steadfast and bearded; yet to hear
the steak knife sing. the ale—a froth
more bitter than seven whorish tongues.

I will have your child and when it comes
you shall take it to the place of your choosing
but bid you no more from me. That child being
the piece You own   [of me].

details are predictable, not to expose the day.

> *What I want, as impractical as it seems, is one*
> *pair of blue velvet socks and a matching purse.*

28

Oh Jane, make haste like Mary and we'll be green for a new hour

But first to deal with the circumference of the arm and not that
straight line on the wrist, a privileged marker—

Rahab hangs a crimson cord in my bedroom window
at my mother's request. The women say
I will find G-d along the highways, but nothing:
Volkswagen shifting; fine driving but
my father, superior. We call him Mario Andretti.

Some call G-d 'Our Father' and 'the Mighty Three.' But
shifting

29

already in the eye and I take to thinking

already mecca and jerusalem hang in the mind of the wayfarer

already we make shadows of our liquid assets. and burn...

already

something dies.

already we have discovered that hope and possibility are not the same.

*　　　*　　　*

already there are captives and captive imaginations.

already and innately there is a spaceman high in a concrete world

already a procession of soldier boys and
girls.

dear already
there flows by bourbon river

banks. of memory. of

dear wherever
thou art and I am not.

breath my
only optimism and

you are and I am not

able
to comb this
disheveled
state of hair.

31

to fill a page, not a person   w/
(& to calm [these] febrile fingers)

far too
inappropriate desires.

all errant

      and the order of the world

momentarily, monumentally lucid, &

      like

            pools of haste

            restrained.

*   *   *

*   *   *

it stands and is dormant today

I am an American, goddamn—
a once & still colorful nation.

the land. zoning. purple. majesty. crowns us all

the word is a likeness:

liberties. libertine.

32 [the doubting number]

Mary my muse   why
has our sisterhood become so estranged.

If I forget thee,

during the film I want to cry out in the blue light, but cannot.

let my right hand forget her cunning.

36

Dear Lover, I have always heard you
[

                              ]

was it   a moment off-shaped
composure when adagio colors slur
or the knocking rhythm of Samoan tattooing—
sound to visible line   warble,
                         flex into timbre

or let me set my humors straight.

                                        *

I held sheers
because my great grandfather was a barber
                                        Pose the apparent nude.

[and]

you who have seen me weep too often

                    we lie in a hopeful city.

37 [Danielle Collobert]

She told the tale of instants...But behind the parabolas generated by certain axioms of impossibility, (of face, of name, of road), behind the confusion of an 'I' hounded by its ordinary and grammatical signals of identity, not really singular nor plural, nor masculine, feminine, something waits fourteen years to speak out against identical neutrality of abyss, as if the mute double of this prose had long been preparing to meet the unverifiable, death.—Jacques Roubaud [trans. Norma Cole]

when this age is reached, and one is still beautiful
but refuses to accept
it then

after the body has flung its soul without exit

I do not know by what method, but certainly
by volition   took all of oneself in a solitary final act

give him the old sword,
the sonar swinging
chink in the armour
glitch in the amour

I am not weary of monitors, he says

pack away your books, profanities abound

shimmer on the rocks
quickly transforms:

bastard urging onward a makeshift barricade.
the student soldiers say

>   *we cannot break from assonance*

like unto prayer, fear dynamic
movement on the water
turtles turning tilapia
ocean shallows to ocean depths.
the sailors say
>   *hold to rhythmic Poseidon*

to circumnavigate this blue globe.
at the dinner party
we eat trout, bang drums against the winter night.

39

Graceless the thorny beard of politic—

                                                Pilate

shadow of his words upon a million tongues

                                              dreaming

*

                                              blasphemy

stage hand, right

                                     deus ex machina

Figure of
                a tu-key in a tent
        [or]
                a turkey in a bottle
        [or]
                a person thinking.

41

What they tell me I do
not know, am scant of their memory
like memories un-had.
stationary head pills and
phone peals   the working nominal.
He in revision. this is not a cigarette-less language or
transfer. automobile the forced capital jesus.
dear R— am I become a fail-
ing thing as the
light remains—orange
a glow

42

quietly on the quadrangle, quiet   a bang—
napoleon   your stead
fast   but the boots
o Wellington   let us explicate.

                                                    this is not a story

begin again in the place of all wars—damnéd

or:

tender to be defeat.

44

tempered already

there in a way—such as little quiver and rivulet conversations.

    electric we say and

I will a certain movement

a way.

this is the part of the opera when...

[she said] *a beautiful work of a beautiful work.*

        ...Octavian becomes Augustus.

45

if there be sandalwood and myrrh

        encounter some greater or lesser thing

                or past   the cedars of lebanon:

        notation beyond trees
though beginning there in a garden of sorts

                the ecstatic and
uncomfortable screaming
             how
               horse remembering
a thesis or something

how many times   *the blessed*

46

is there need of prologue or
dear husband   stretched this place has taken two
of our young'uns. it is not the miles but schismatic   [range].
yours is in the invariable motion and same silent cunning.
I liked being called mister. our shocked fichus
dead in the hole of this place—the kitchen a considerable hospice—
but how it must have missed your green hands. whimper of fallen
leaves.

48

Dear Friend   how I am certain that months have passed
and my zebra plant has died.
the afternoons here are   stark without him,
little zebra. Socrates died too.
one must keep this in mind.
I'd rather not think about _____   [—]

soul sisters had not ought to be so
estranged. verily, my dear, but do offer exceptions to the rule
where the err, would not establish culpability
between fish and once-flowering plants.
double-space. sloppier as
the year progresses   period after.
pare the gap, its pomegranate shape.
sirens and prophetic agendas/
a chromosomal landscape emerges to rent
again.   once-bloomed.

49

there alone
wrestled a man until dawn

some herculean effort

harvest moon

      and her incessant
      blood-letting of the world

55

muse, you and what soldiers do you keep?
white sky—what battle:
nights pass with the same lethargic slur as days.

empire holy and fat as Roman.
so much currency.
the many graves.
and the children to come.

56

dear You   you and your mercenary boots, how they march on and on
and and and
reside in me. punishment for a tyrant heart. but

from the street stoop, other television lit rooms—
dark but for the blue. husbands keeping the secrets of their
best friends from their wives. whose wives. theirs.

because *I am* I would want those things, he says.
besides, there is an agreement. the pelvis is not settled.

                              what wonders there are.

is it so easy, god killer?

i was that god. augustus.

57

i was that god-killer. i.
memories   barbs and wire fence.

god-killer. i.

the spirit flinging.

59

the letter reads: *be mine, like a possession be.*
conveys a passion. alas...
still a hoyden i see, she says   with grace.

stormy monday.now this, break in heat but
sick hue of green.

Dear Elizabeth*********I suppose that being your sister you will allow me this
liberty.

disaster in the sense that the stars went amiss.
roust antony's fleet, by midday shall we conquer the sea.
our day delivered up by cleopatra's dead pan face.
give to Caesar what is Caesar's.

may we be so bold as to say:

a hero can, in the end, only give his life. and heroine, hers.

60

going against the rhythms of speech

i used to not be this way—

this way.

a pleasure in the drowning

for a time in
a place.

i am no longer that place.

now this   other rhetoric.

mercurial discontent. it is
difficult to make a distinction
between possibility and its opposite

as the organism rises to
its fevered pitch sable stasis—the

calm. or

rock and roll evangelist. let it go.
let it go, motherfucker.

but pressed into finitude

the sky turns again, again, again dis-
heartened eye looking at the moon,
or whatever can be made out
of celestial bodies.

the sensation is the same here,
and what ought to protect me against
too much motion is itself a gentle motion.

it is the same here, the knowledge of
self and world.

whatever city i am—lovecraft was providence.

so come, distill me

again, i am so

silent
yet can be a pure act.
and you
have gathered my bourbon lilies or

whatever the muses allow, my dear,

they will.

is this the point
where memory stand-ins operate in the mind
of the reader or
of the author.

when a writer, or any reader for that matter, begins
to inhabit the world, a world...

leaves some residue
for instance, when my hypos gets such that i
want to knock people's hats off.

or that, in orgasm, to think of the body electric.
alternating current/ disconnected current.

61

stability come

a tower build...sybarite, oh—

say so in the dark
room, midnight psychobabble in ear

barnacle brain and brooklyn below
the borough, here—my finger deep into queens.

enter down a pitch stair
and discover this man

this man of gaunt stature
undoubtedly with van dyke beard   [...]

sometimes sappho, fragmentary speech off what was surely
a mobile tongue.

this age has crept upon me when others of my kingdom...

62

[to the addressee—]

if we don't have the body, let us apply our hands and tongues to language. alas,

april is the cruellest month, echo, echo
from the many crests of undulating thought.

speak now, or delay the process.
echo the very best guttural, the
intoned breathing—somewhat expressive and
meritoriously articulate in its own right. it says yes
at times, once one is forced into the drama   [...]

attachment: is that

deta*ched attachment* or *attached detachment* or what

when the connotation seems so vex some.

when transitive verb, in the passive,
commonly followed by *to,*

am attached to, for instance, meaning—
a fondness, some type of devotion, or so the dictionary says.

but lacking the grace,
barking cur at my nature
[not my, not I].

63

rhythmic and yet not constant pale flashings against dun walls.

the onlooker sees
despondency   where also there is

jubilation of sorts.

and yet not hidden

according to Immanuel [Kant]:
the day is beautiful, and the night—sublime.

by both *lux* and shade—
supplications.

65

bitter root and remnant.

oh jonah, come out of the belly of the whale, my love
and leave the carcass on the shoreline.

ye men for bone & oil.

like some Ishmael tossed on the seas,
indeed, we are no strangers to vulgarity.

66

dear Amerigo Vespucci, on dubious authority
draw the boundaries of my body—
these hips like the South American mainland.

do it, brother, so i'll take sketchy root, so i'll be made new.

69

Ishmael, my beauty

      born of concubine womb.

      then to be driven into wilderness, not quite set free
      years later to appear in a whale battered sea.

my lord, where have you been.
sitting amongst those who would make catamites of young boys?

and everywhere, gored by bullish things:

      love thine enemy.

      lie down in the waters of thine enemy.

nothing to return; nothing to assemble.

and at the end, to merely allude.

what does it take to drown
a man[Q]   a self[Q].

the only one of my hands.

70

inversion paralysis

pain in the shoulder and collarbone, peter bookeater.

lowghost moving   in/out

of [   ]

canaries and other yellow birds.

tense attempt between   assertion or articulation.

significance
of any letter; of any body of letters.

stasis: myriad redundancies forcing on sphere, as if to demonstrate motion.

a force, harbor upon breast.

71

fear was this dream's accomplice.
confession: I had been tasting myself for months.

from the Brooklyn rooftop
I desire nothing but the absent
presence of *you*—the indefinable
faceless you, my love:
> *[in medias lumen, dies. pt. 1.*

>> *judah, my hope, draw me a map of palestine and let us*
>> *settle this matter with the children of ishmael and esau.*

>> *come   let us speak with our brother israel—be like aaron be.*

>> *map: judah after the fall of israel. what i mean to say is that*
>> *my ire has expired as a state [of being].*

>> *dear judah, we looked for you to come out of the rain [thursday]*
>> *but you did not yet come.*

>> *judah, my hesed, I looked for you today*
>> *by the seashore at coney island.*

>> *judah, let us be bookmakers.*

>> *we live outside   judah.*
>> *peace comes after the anger is exhausted. but collective, transgressions*
>> *of the fathers into the third and fourth generations.*

>> *from this little emperor: waterloo and everything after—   ...]*

and there among the gentle fairies,
and with pregnant sonja down below,
and Colin getting drunker by the quarter hour—

I asserted nothing save my substantial abstinence

judah   come, let us glorify.

72

in the heart there is no murmur.

we shift parallax; we shift semantic directions
and, belaboring the point, overstretch the delineated
circumference of squirrel.

I have a rodent heart.

with my incisors so long, you are marked for
verbatim read-backs, relentless

yet now in absentia of the vicious cycle.

I am quiet under sheets   [which is perhaps a lie].

I have not laughed in years   [also a lie].

I am under the river, swollen

prideful and Quaker lust, wander-
lust.

These are my hands. my fingers are the body's own heartbreak.

73

between the words and the markers and the inks and the screens,
between the public and the private and the casual and the intimate,
between the world and the world projected, between the dream and the thought

there is some civic duty in *this.*

the individual & the writing & the

love that courageous act—yes, in all directions

       we [begin to] see.

APOLOGIES: DRAFTS 75—123

for Rosmarie Waldrop

75

oh my sabellian heart.

he stands—as if to illustrate the metaphor—on the bathtub ledge, curved
under arch of foot. he is hanging on

to the metal rod and looks out the window.

as the act complete, he falls downward smacking heels against
bare white tiles.

scene: i love you too much and

i do not love ...

cast out—   my name is
legion, to the swine

76

listless. language-less in the moment
at the bar

in spirits the
reservoir of hubris, gushes but

if by memory alone the musculature senses
what is

remainder and
what is not

then

again

today I could not bear
watching news coverage
of a dog

gassed.

and when i turn
i know that,
Oh Owen, it is not particularly at all *Dulce et decorum est pro patria mori!*

78

63° September. *this is love* or *inconsistency in the atmosphere.*
one cannot be alone—whore of Babylon at my door. Semeirimus and her

                              garden delight.

hope—a foiled aether. body of evaporating liquid.

frightened by the smoke: purple plumage, purple robe, purple flowers.
never a wedding girl

the ecstatic linkage,
          fill of void.

[this is] any life. the *anywhere* of locale, of being.
it is not *my life,* rather

                         a life.

                 &

people change and

people don't change.

79

You give and you give. you give when you do not want to give.
you give you give. you give when you do not want to give.

Because I am more than just myself. I am my dreaming self
getting better at this.
—Sarah Gambito, Untitled

end of anchorage = death by hallucination   or to

stumble across

revelation which is not 'mine'
is not

revelation   gradual procession of irony
                                                                    `

to actualize any potential
one stumbles against

'impossibility'. something always looming, the world a

tapestry of uncertain fiber[s].

80 *for kathleen andersen*

[this is the apology]   for union square.

for beauty exhaled. hope's beginning to

                                        perish.

vast gaps

                                              in undertones

transfer from english to english

by way of

                                        yelling

godammit to the open sky
only
                                        to disturb

a homeless man sleeping at the Union Square subway station.

i thought of my weakness, sister,
and how my
paranoia whispered: you are in danger
                               of becoming and being

                               a civilian/a
citizen.

pt. 2

sometimes i

pretend to be an active member
of society

                                         fingers ensuing euphoria

                                         out of many   one

e pluribus unum

"one out of many" "we hold

these truths   to be self-evident."

this pax Americana, like an empire in decline, balloons unfavorably

it is better here, but so often divided as to stalemate. & we are just
citizens.

82

elixir   exiler

cannot decide between two terms, as in   malaise-ennui

memory   quixotic quests, percival searching

                                              is it resolved ?

submission service

or, the girls thought something by which they'd been infected

or by

my ordinary fury nevertheless unleashed, not yet
so thought
an alacrity without lucid skin

the membrane in between my legs

i wanted nothing realistic or

                                        undefined

83

if it's a cu[n]t it should be healed

keen and penetrating, my name

"wrapped in your skin"

                              ***

                                                    here   here

in sanctity of township

                                        [a] delineation by size

little elm city = the getaway

for a moment   for morning   [for having too many tears]

the night before, cozy

                    soporific conversations. in the orange
                    fabric, a rusting draw to lounge

& then:

                    I dreamt of something and I

                         cannot recall

84

i'd want to feel you not

you, drunk, feeling me.

> i have to come to terms with the fact that the *operative*
> *phrase* is "ought to"
>
> as in the jamesian notion that "there *ought to* be a
> moral equivalent to war."

i'm telling you that humility and humiliation are not
my strong suits and so

—coiled into a taut muscle—

you see my viper fury

moving against the linear   *feel you not*

                                   ought to

have no fear of negative space.

> just walk with me a little

> while.

promise me
there is no eschatological future

aberration

& musing on

celebrity, diplomacy, supremacy—the question of

the commoner. little poet. little little boots.

hypocrite   like everybody else

pulsing in the spot

light all around   we dance on pages.

87

Thus have I had thee as a dream doth flatter,
In sleep a king, but in waking no such matter.
—Wm. Shakespeare, Sonnet 87

you see, I want impossible things   ...

supplication:

can't go
backwards or forwards

            ,

and the voice is home. like sirens/not like sirens. the name is home. &
home remains unknown.

mind striking out into abstract space[s],   abstract bodies
                                                            of alphabet

again malady, spreads. is not cancer. not wholly

                                        physical.

but spreads, yes

                        no blank pages

                                                my mother crying

despondent distances
we'll recover one life after another

88

tired and hungry, and in need of water—

words fill out

                                         a dull body of pen scratches

luminaries. you are any one of some extreme.

and listen, listen to the thudding sound, as it
acquires too much meaning

91

do you look so royal now

arctic thrust   this January lacking any delicate banter
silence   the cold

and brutal

libido

harbored between 27° and the East River

92

discontent and winter and me back again.

you're in the middle of it before you realize that

it's a major storm. an event, historical. momentous

bitter snow. *hold me up when I am such a shiver and shy smile*

93

the nature of immediacy

[

taps on my window in winter glazing
light is blue or yellow and I yawn to each, either waking or waning

]

burrows deeper, a song in my wilderness

and rise and rise

yet there remains the whole quotidian aspect of living

study notes:

over time, subject developed a symbiotic relationship with the television.

damnably.

I will not   rest with the lyric   alone.

circle back. rhythm. again.

94 for Oregon

perilous vast — this juncture of boroughs between us.

                              as much
                              affinity for mountains as for the sea.

and listen, listen to the thudding sound

                         [acquired too much meaning]

hungry and tired and in need of water.

                         how would you speak of yr future?

         I don't know — the only
foreign tongue I know
is my longing.

                         [something that 'gestures' toward]

95

this yr is harder than the yr before:

gripped in the clutch of

        terror the

long winter   a gauzy sun rising
to warm us   so little

                        [hope is not everlasting]

your god will exact upon you vengeance

realness residual

form the words of an evangelist:
        America my beauty   be not savage for blood lust in the guise
        of false righteousness

          and I am with you.

I—am [h]er i can

        be liberty

97

allah akbar: 'god is great'

all night long I lay longwise and not

  sat up and paced, at intervals always
  thinking of war, now, war and fire

        ['failed' diplmacy, or 'the feigned diplomacy'
        having expired...]

& locate hope in the space between

nausea: 'the will of god'

98

it is sometimes bad to sleep. to dream. the American dream

obscured.

[and still you seek]

diplomacy

overtly a

'war for peace'

and still you seek

.

.

100

the price of awareness is nearly insufferable

at times, coming to no opinion.

one tries to see both sides of various contexts

—afterall, there are two I's in my *praenomen.*

two eyes in the heady head   and

always the risk of 'damage' and 'concussion'

after any 'breakdown'—however minor—

whatever gets you through the night

soldier/civilian

[you are in danger of *becoming*]

101

how to locate

     a vacant

  hope

     in the 'palimpsest'

i have implored those living beauties

                           [from time to time]
     and received not some benefit

but only you here as

     'groove dreams whipped stiff'

all your translations [between languages, within sonic color fields or in images so] are not inspiration but the air itself

     gifts afforded by knowledge

upon the worthy

      [though who, the worthy]

stumble upon

and be pleased
    an interchange.

on the outside, and vast though the afternoon

         may   be

exclusion

the referent, saddened.

we play out this word onward and wish our bicycles could
fly. to the lunar realm like when we were children—

still seeking out space, the frontier beyond
the moon, where surely what is lost may be found
again perhaps   intact

and falls, the body in gravity's grave enticement

but, accordingly fossorial—burrowing trenches in the 'social scene' in
the domicile, in great desert

what fortitude it takes to breathe

some centrifugal displacement from 'the vortex'

Caligula waits.

103

[there 'liberty' in dis: connect.] in

                open possibilities

morning 3 juli: transgressing 'the Law.'

If not for me America i think
you are in decline. still the wyoming green turf

what is it, really, to have said:

      I sent you, in contemporary
      wor[l]ds—we stutter the strutter or do not speak

(how)[ever]

[already we have learned that hope and possibility are not the same.]

and things appropriate to nothing are nothing

                              it's a down/ and

/ /...../ /......./ /......./././ / / / / / / / / / /......./ /

                              and a stroke

and must quiet this 'hasten'

and so a great sacrifice made: olympia DeLuxe

109 *for the Graces*

i love my neighbors.

things happen. we
make mistakes. we

meet ourselves for the first time, again

a wound. things happen.

seek a locality, a life

& empathy &

[rest]

& what the music wants is

what the music always wants

117

your *godot* is always a woman

and she will not come.

though she should, in a way, not

to save

you

but to
open the pages of your book

sequestered and meaningful the wet depth of

a wish list

the 'expressible' which I try to impress upon you

shadow to the inexpressible

this utterance, dancing around while

the inexpressible middle is
trial by

fire.   [any fan is   merely

pseudo-cool]

120

no incendiary

                                                     devices.

it's not as much as a conundrum

                                            as it is

love not

                                  rancor

succulent babes, o! ever a fever gone, wild & oaten

            to trap the preposition

not by perfidy

*   *   *   *

                                      where are dark
lines visible in

                      the solar specter, i recall the

       invariable

                            o wayfarer

       listless though you light

                    out upon the prairie of

which i know nothing.

                                  otherwise, i am

truly beyond

            words

121 *for mr shivery*

transmission long, farewell through static

barking though the dog soon lay still

[i beg of you to burn it down, transfer me onto glass plates &]

122

the thought interrupted: *you just let me worry about verbosity.*

my straw man argument, haunted. among
plenty of shade, discomfort still as
in/(or for example) recurring dreams

  that resolve but… brought so low, so low to say

          i hope you can keep yr
          head above the rain

  if it weren't so overcast my thinking
might not be so clouded

(with) the enormity of my heavings –O—

blunt reality,

sometimes even then light of day. what,
say Schubert? what say?

123 *for Melissa Van Doren*

after Emily D.

that formal feeling, and then so much

reeling. the pitch & peak, the ornery

senses. great magnitude and shifts
of state.

of one thousand trampled desires

i confuse savory & sultry

i wish i could get enough into the stupor
as to begin the letting go…

i wish the stupor would come &

let me go

124

purge[d]. or perjury in the small
cardiac of our affections

where now our behavioral vortex, cortex & cortez.
this exploration proceeds.
          [this—demonstrative]. as of, goddam this stillborn heart.

          *   *   *   *

musket rhetoric & liberation pois
                            ed or
                            oned

                pardon & pardoned

          made eyes at the signpost &
                        died there in a way

beside the mandevela, issuing
                a train of fuscia bursts
                                  you looked gallant
underneath the water tower

************************ [but]

somewhere beneath the pedestal from which i had
        fallen
                my shattered**********lay glimmering.

*   *   *   *

opine my opinion o my eye in & out of focus.

125

ever pernicious, here our estuary dries &
forms a stain

preference for the illuminated

                          i have given over my
                  complexity, complexities

          to make your acquaintance i have followed
a trail into a thicket

126

      & i miss you a terrible storm   my eye   a fierce grip

so easily   . apparently affected, you could not allow me

emotion without sarcasm   imagine

consequently that your thought orchard

bear much fruit

&   gardening   the verbiage, these weedy plots

128

if not for lack of vision but still you lost
creature: clever complicity upbraids the dogwood
branches

129

you were a singer but now
you croon, husky, the liquid of your honey
tongue turned arid, & still they love you more

have made of you a diva

you cover yourself. you cover, you take cover

131

America—oh, my

     love, we are to fall,

          my love

& i will sing of you while it

     rains and rains and how

our reign draws closer down

          into the recessed

          into the change.

BIOGRAPHICAL NOTE:

Kristin P. Bradshaw is a language artist who also works with collage, photography and soundscapes. Her poems have appeared in magazines like the *New Orleans Review, New American Poetry, Chase Park,* and *No: a Journal of the Arts.* Her letterpress chapbook and audio CD, *The Difficult Nature ~~of Contemplation~~,* is forthcoming from Tiger Food Press / Percival House. She holds an MFA from Brown University, an MA in Religion from Yale Divinity School, and now teaches in the Writing Program of Pacific Northwest College of Art in Portland, Oregon.

This book was designed and computer typeset in 10 pt. Palatino, with Herculaneum titles, by Rosmarie Waldrop. Printed on 55 lb. Writers' Natural (an acid-free paper), smyth-sewn and glued into paper covers by McNaugthon & Gunn in Saline, Michigan. The cover by the author uses Lucida Grande lettering. There are 600 copies.